SALVATION REVELATION

The Rock-Solid Salvation and the Alien Within

GRU FREE

WESTBOW
PRESS®
A DIVISION OF THOMAS NELSON
& ZONDERVAN

WestBow Press books may be ordered through booksellers or by contacting:

WestBow Press
A Division of Thomas Nelson & Zondervan
1663 Liberty Drive
Bloomington, IN 47403
www.westbowpress.com
844-714-3454

Scriptures taken from the Holy Bible, New International Version®, NIV®.
Copyright © 1973, 1978, 1984, 2011 by Biblica, Inc.™ Used by permission
of Zondervan. All rights reserved worldwide. www.zondervan.com The
"NIV" and "New International Version" are trademarks registered in
the United States Patent and Trademark Office by Biblica, Inc.®

ISBN: 978-1-6642-0901-5 (sc)
ISBN: 978-1-6642-0902-2 (e)

Library of Congress Control Number: 2020920185

Print information available on the last page.

WestBow Press rev. date: 10/16/2020

This work is dedicated to those who are off balance in their relationship with Christ. I mean those who are never quite confident about their salvation from one day to the next and are unsure if they have done enough. To those who have no assurance of their salvation and to those who want a closer walk with the Lord, not based on fear, but faith, beginning with the knowledge that in Christ, we are free to serve the Lord as the people he created us to be. Some preach as if the church and believers were going to be condemned with the world if they did not measure up. And that is not going to happen. This is God's church, his house. We are God's building, his family for whom Jesus died and rose.

Lift up your eyes to the heavens, and look at the earth beneath: for the heavens shall vanish like smoke, and the earth will wear out like a garment, and its inhabitants die like flies. But my salvation will last forever, my righteousness will never fail.

—Isaiah 51:6

God never promised us tomorrow, but he did promise us forever: eternity.

CONTENTS

PREFACE

WITH SO MANY VOICES IN the world and takes on the afterlife, there are many—even among Christians—who are thoroughly confused as to what the truth is and where they might stand. They include those who come out of Mormonism, Islam, Jehovah's Witness, Buddhism, and others. They come from different denominations, such as Pentecostalism, Catholicism, Baptists, the Amish, and Congregationalism. However, we all have two things in common: Jesus and the Word of God.

If we have come to know Jesus through belief in the truth and have placed our faith in him, the Word of God says what it says to us all. My hope is that this short book may clarify some things for the saints of God and give a deeper insight into God's eternal salvation.

ABRAHAM AT THE FEAST

BY FAITH

THE WORD SAYS, "THE SPIRITUAL did not come first, but the natural, and after that the spiritual" (1 Corinthians 15:46). So first, we are going to take a look at salvation from the Old Testament. That is, how the Old Testament saints were made righteous and saved. We look at it in the natural, where it will be understood in the Spirit. And then we bring it into the New Testament.

After this, the word of the Lord came to Abram in a vision:

> "Do not be afraid, Abram. I am your shield, your very great reward."
>
> But Abram said, "O sovereign Lord, what can you give me since I remain childless and the one who will inherit my estate is Eliezer of Damascus?" And Abram said, "You have given me no children; so a servant in my household will be my heir.
>
> Then the word of the Lord came to him: "This man will not be your heir, but a son coming," from your own body will be your heir. "He took him outside and said, "Look up at the heavens and count

the stars-if indeed you can count them." Then he said to him, " So shall your offspring be."

Abram believed the Lord, and he credited to him as righteousness. (Genesis 15:1–6)

Righteousness was credited to Abram entirely based on his faith, his believing God. Though Abram and Sarai had wanted children for many years but were not able to produce, he chose to believe God. Even now that they were old and past the years—it would seem—of natural childbirth.

The explanation, validation, and confirmation of this covenant comes in Genesis 17:9–14:

> Then God said to Abraham, "As for you, you must keep my covenant, you and your descendants after you for the generations to come. This is my covenant with you and the generations after you, the covenant you are to keep: Every male among you shall be circumcised. You are to undergo circumcision and it will be the sign of the covenant between me and you. For the generations to come every male among you who is eight days old must be circumcised, including those born in your household or bought with money from a foreigner-those who are not your offspring. Whether born in your household or bought with your money, they must be circumcised. My covenant in your flesh is to be an everlasting covenant. Any uncircumcised male, who has not been circumcised, will be cut off from his people; he has broken my covenant."

No male is exempt from circumcision. The eighth day speaks of new beginnings, which stands for the day a person is circumcised in heart by the Spirit and enters life. A person who has never made the decision to believe and trust God will be cut off from those who have, including family, for flesh and blood cannot enter the kingdom of God. Only those born of the Spirit can do so.

> On that very day Abraham took his son Ishmael and all those born in his household or bought with money, every male in his household, and circumcised them, as God told him. (Genesis 17:23)

Abraham wasted no time.

The explanation and fulfillment of this are found in the New Testament, as we shall see.

Romans 2:28–29 tells us, "A man is not a Jew if he is only one outwardly, nor is circumcision merely outward and physical. No, a man is a Jew if he is one in inwardly, and circumcision is circumcision of the heart, by the Spirit, not the written code. Such a man's praise is not from men, but from God."

So circumcision in the flesh was a forerunner of the true circumcision, that of the heart by the Spirit through faith. This happens immediately when a person—male or female—turns to the Lord. Until that time we are blind to the things of God because the flesh is of the natural realm, and the Spirit is of the spiritual realm, two different kingdoms.

> Even to this day when Moses is read, a veil covers their hearts. But whenever anyone turns to the Lord the veil is taken away. Now the Lord is the Spirit, and where the Spirit of the Lord is, there is freedom. (2 Corinthians 3:15–17)

Circumcision by the Spirit is the removal or the cutting away of sin nature, the veil that keeps all unbelievers blind to the things of God.

> For we maintain that a man is justified by faith
> apart from observing the law. Is God the God of
> the Jews only? Is he not the God of the Gentiles
> to? Yes, of Gentiles too, since there is only one
> God, who will justify the circumcised by faith
> and the uncircumcised through that same faith.
> (Romans 3:28–30)

Jews and Gentiles (a Gentile is anyone who is not a Jew) alike are justified, made righteous by God through faith in him.

Circumcision of the flesh was a seal and marked the person as belonging to God. The person was now an heir to faith, but not guaranteeing that a person actually had saving faith as did Abraham.

> What then shall we say that Abraham, our forefather,
> discovered in this matter? If, in fact Abraham was
> justified by works, he had something to boast about-
> but not before God. What does the scripture say?
> "Abraham believed God and it was credited to him
> as righteousness." (Romans 4:1–3)

There are many who attempt to blend works and faith—being saved by faith through grace and being kept by works, or some variation thereof. Abraham's faith alone was credited as righteousness.

> I would like to learn just one thing from you: Did
> you receive the Spirit by observing the law, or by
> believing what you heard? Are you so foolish? After
> beginning with the Spirit, are you now trying to
> attain your goal by human effort? Have you suffered
> so much for nothing- if it really was for nothing?
> Does God give you his Spirit and work miracles
> among you because you observe the law, or because
> you believe what you heard (the gospel).

Consider Abraham: "He believed God, and it was credited to him as righteousness. Understand then, those that believe are children of Abraham. (Galatians 3:2–7)

Some have said that when Abraham offered Isaac on the altar, combined with his believing God concerning his descendants, produced God's response concerning righteousness.

Well the time line does not fit because Abraham was between seventy-five and eighty-six years old when he received that credit from God. And Abraham was one hundred when Isaac was born. Then give Isaac a few years to grow. It was probably another thirty or so years from the time Abraham initially received the credit before they, Isaac and Abraham, traveled to Mount Mariah to sacrifice Isaac.

And he received the sign of circumcision a seal of the righteousness that he had by faith while he was still uncircumcised. (Romans 4:11)

In other words, that was a sign or testament to the fact that Abraham had faith. He was a believer in God and believed his Word, and God sealed his righteousness, making Abraham his possession. And God credited Abraham with righteousness, or made Abraham righteous on credit, looking forward to a future event when the credit would become a gift—the event being the death and resurrection of Jesus Christ, the Son of God. By his sacrifice, Jesus paid the debt for sin. Everyone who looks to the Son and believes in him is given the gift of righteousness, life, through their faith in him.

For my father's will is that everyone who looks to the Son and believes in him shall have eternal life, and I will raise him up at the last day. (John 6:40)

The will of God is looking to Jesus.

> The world and its desires pass away, but the man who does the will of God lives forever. (1 John 2:17)

Application of the seal is taught in several places in the New Testament.

> Now it is God who makes both us and you stand firm in Christ. He anointed us, set his "seal of ownership" on us, and put his Spirit in our hearts as a deposit, guaranteeing what is to come. (2 Corinthians 1:21)

> Now it is God who has made us for this very purpose and has given us the Spirit as a deposit, guaranteeing what is to come. (2 Corinthians 5:5)

> And you also were included in Christ when you heard the word of truth, the gospel of your salvation. Having believed you were marked in him with a seal, the promised Holy Spirit who is a deposit guaranteeing our inheritance until the redemption of those who are God's possession-to the praise of his glory. (Ephesians 1:13–14)

Being included in Christ happened when you heard the gospel and believed it. Most of us heard the message many times before making a decision for Christ. Some of us made that decision at the altar in church. Some made it in a restaurant, others at home or in a car. One young man said that he was saved on first base. Another person was saved in the restroom of a McDonald's restaurant. No matter when or where we received the Lord, we were immediately forgiven, filled with the Spirit, sealed, and then readied to experience that great release and peace given by the Spirit of Christ. In the gospels, Jesus said, "Let the children come to me," so the sooner we come to the Lord, the better.

Think about it this way. When you buy a car, a house, or some other expensive item, you put down a deposit until you come back and complete the deal. We gave God no deposit because we did not buy our way in. God gave us a deposit based on our faith in believing his Word, the gospel. The Holy Spirit is God, so we might say that God gave us God as a deposit guaranteeing what God was going to do. And that guarantees our future in Christ.

We can assume that God has never lost a deposit. That being the case neither has he lost anyone that he has given it to. Neither has he ever canceled his promise to anyone, taken back his deposit, and turned a believer over to be condemned.

> And do not grieve the Holy Spirit of God, with whom you were sealed for the day of redemption. (Ephesians 4:30)

> Nevertheless, God's solid foundation stands firm, sealed with this inscription: "The Lord knows those who are his," and, "Everyone who confesses the name of the Lord must turn away from wickedness. (2 Timothy 2:19)

And how does God know or remember those who are his? "Those who obey his commands live in him, and he in them. And this is how we know that he lives in us: We know it by the Spirit by the Spirit he gave us" (1 John 3:24).

> Consider Abraham: "He believed God, and it was credited to him as righteousness." Understand that those who believe are children of Abraham. (Believers one and all). The scripture foresaw that God would justify the gentiles by faith, and announced the gospel in advance to Abraham: "All nations will be blessed through you." So those who

have faith are blessed along with Abraham, the man
of faith. (Galatians 3:6–9)

When Jesus had entered Capernaum, a centurion
came to him, asking for help. "Lord," he said, "my
servant lies home paralyzed and in terrible suffering."
Jesus said to him, "I will go and heal him."
The centurion replied, "Lord, I do not deserve
to have you come under my roof. But just say the
word, and my servant will be healed. For I myself
are a man under authority, with soldiers under
me. I tell this one, Go, and he goes; and that one,
Come, and he comes. I say to my servant, Do this,
and he does it."
When Jesus heard this, he was astonished and
said to those following him, "I tell you the truth,
I have not found anyone in Israel with such great
faith. I say to you that many will come from the
east and the west, and take their places "at the feast
with Abraham, Isaac, and Jacob in the kingdom of
heaven." (Matthew 8:5–11)

By faith he made his home in the promised land like
a stranger in a foreign country: he lived in tents, "as
did Isaac and Jacob, who were heirs with him of the
same promise." (Hebrews 11:9)

So we can say that Abraham, Isaac, and Jacob received salvation
by faith, having been made righteous on credit. That credit
of righteousness was a loan until the Righteous One came and
accomplished salvation. The credit was viable and interest-free for
two thousand years, more or less. The credit was good for as long as
it needed to be. And at the proper time, the credit of righteousness
was counted as a gift.

THE EXODUS

INSTRUCTIONS THROUGH MOSES—THE MESSAGE

> The Lord said to Moses and Aaron in Egypt, "This month is to be for you the first month, the first month of your year. Tell the whole community of Israel that on the 10th day of this month each man is to take a lamb for his family, one for each house hold."
>
> —Exodus 12:1–3

NO REASON WAS GIVEN FOR taking the lamb. Taking the lamb was by faith in obedience to the Word of the Lord. No part of the community was exempt. Everyone to whom the Word came needed to choose his lamb.

"The Gospel was announced in advance to Abraham" (Galatians 3:38). And the gospel, meaning good news, is given here to the children of Israel.

> The animals you choose must be year-old males without defect, and you may take them from the

9

> sheep or the goats. Take care of them until the
> fourteenth day of the month, when all the people
> of the community of Israel must slaughter them at
> twilight. Then they are to take some of the blood and
> put on the sides and tops of the door frames of the
> houses where they eat the lambs. (Exodus 12:5–7)

"The animals you choose must be year-old males without defect."
The instructions are given as to what lamb is acceptable to the Lord:
One that is young and in perfect health. And you are responsible
for the choice. Jesus was young and in perfect health. And Jesus was
not a goat but a lamb.

If you choose a goat, you may choose a Gentile, a Joseph Smith,
a Mohammad, or maybe Buddha, none of which would be any
help at all.

The entire community was responsible for slaughtering their
individual lambs at twilight. As each one of us, every single person
on planet Earth, aided in putting Jesus to death. The Jews rejected
him, and the Gentiles crucified him. He was put to death for our
sins, and he was made alive by the Spirit. Jesus died at the end of
the day he was crucified.

The Jews were just as guilty of sin as the Egyptians; there is no
one righteous, not even one (Romans 3:10). The reason God chose
the Jews rather than the Egyptians or anyone else was because he
loved them, and he had a plan. Other than that, who really knows?
God, by his own authority and purpose, does what he wants when
he wants.

> This is how you are to eat it: with your cloak
> tucked into your belt, your sandals on your feet
> and your staff in your hand. Eat it in haste; it is
> the Lord's Passover.
> On that same night I will pass through Egypt
> and strike down every first born-both men and

animals-and I will bring judgment on all the Gods of Egypt. I am the Lord. The blood will be a sign for you on the houses where you are; and when I see the blood, I will pass over you. No destructive plague will touch you when I strike Egypt. (Exodus 12:11–13)

Eat the Passover lamb fully dressed and ready to go. Eat it in haste. So soon after you kill the Passover lamb, and you apply the blood, your enemy, the one who held you in bondage, is struck, releasing you. The blood will be a sign to you that when I see the blood, I will pass over you. No destructive plague will touch you when I strike Egypt. Why? Because you're covered.

Be dressed and ready to go. Again this is your responsibility. In the natural you dress yourself in earthly rags. However, when we are born of the Spirit, we are immediately dressed in garments of righteousness supplied by God. And with that, we are positioned, given a place in the kingdom of God.

> But because of his great love for us, God, who is rich in mercy, made us alive with Christ even when we were dead in transgressions-it is by grace you have been saved. 6 And God raised us up with Christ and seated us with him in the heavenly realms in Christ Jesus, in order that in the coming ages he might show the incomparable riches of his grace, expressed in his kindness to us in Christ Jesus. (Ephesians 2:4–7)

> Since, then, you have been raised with Christ, set your hearts on things above, where Christ is seated at the right hand of God. Set your minds on things above, not on earthly things. For you died, and your life is now hidden with Christ in God. When Christ who is your life appears, then you also will appear with him in glory. (Colossians 3:1–4)

Now physically we are still on planet Earth. However, in God's plan we are already there in glory, where God has positioned us, having given us a reservation. So he basically says to look for the manifestation of the Kingdom of Heaven, believe in the manifestation of the Kingdom of Heaven, plan on the manifestation of the Kingdom of Heaven, and live your life as if Christ was going to appear today.

THE EVENT

Then Moses summoned all the elders of Israel and said to them, Go at once and select the animals for your families and slaughter the Passover lamb. Take a bunch of hyssop, dip it in the blood in the basin and put some of the blood on the top and on both sides of the door frames. Not one of you shall go out the door of his house until morning, When the Lord goes through the land to strike down the Egyptians, he will see the blood on the top and sides of the door frame and he will pass over that doorway, and he will not permit the destroyer to enter your houses and strike you down.

—Exodus 12:21–23

THE GOSPEL—THAT IS, THE GOOD news—goes out that God has authorized another to take your place when his judgment comes, and his wrath is poured out. His instructions are specific.

1. You believe the gospel.
2. You choose the lamb according to his instructions.
3. You kill the Passover lamb.

4. You apply the blood.

> For the life of a creature is in the blood, and I have
> given it to you to make atonement for yourselves on
> the alter; it is the blood that makes atonement for
> one's life. (Leviticus 17:11)

In Exodus 12:22, "hyssop" represents the Holy Spirit, who
applies the blood the moment we believe. The basin represents the
reservoir of the blood of Christ that never runs dry.

So it's up to us to believe and choose the lamb, the Lamb of God.
The Holy Spirit does the rest.

> The next day John saw Jesus coming toward him
> and said, "Look, the Lamb of God, who takes away
> the sin of the world!" (John 1:29)

THE GOSPEL

JUST THINK HOW IMPORTANT THE gospel is. God announced it to Abraham around four thousand years ago. It was good news then, and it is good news now.

And what was the good news that Abraham received? Let's look at it again:

> Understand, then, that those who believe are children of Abraham. The Scripture foresaw that God would justify the Gentiles by faith, and announced the gospel in advance to Abraham: All nations will be blessed through you. So those who have faith are blessed along with Abraham the man of faith. (Galatians 3:7–9)

"All nations will be blessed through you." Jews, Gentiles, and all who through faith receive God's Word and believe it will be blessed. Abraham had a son, Isaac—who was the child of the promise—who fathered twins, Jacob and Esau. Jacob, whose name was changed to Israel, had twelve sons and one daughter. Israel's son Judah had children, and one of his descendants was King David, and through his line were born Mary and Joseph. Mary gave birth to Jesus, who was fathered by the Spirit of God. This makes Joseph Jesus's stepfather and makes Jesus God's Son and a direct descendant of Abraham. So through Abraham came the Savior of the world. Good news and a blessing to the world.

Isaac is a forerunner of all those who are born of the Spirit. Isaac was born by the power of the Spirit. He was the son promised to Abraham, the child of the promise.

> Now you brothers like Isaac, are children of promise. At that time the son born in the ordinary way (Ishmael) persecuted the son born by the power of the Spirit, (Isaac). (Galatians 3:28–29)

Isaac was born by the power of the Spirit, and we are born again by that same power.

> Now brothers I want to remind you of the gospel I preached to you, which you have received and on which you have taken your stand. "By this gospel you are saved," if you hold firmly to the word I preached to you. Otherwise, you have believed in vain.
>
> For what I received I passed on to you as first importance: that Christ died for our sins according to the Scriptures, and that he was buried, that he was raised on the third day according to the Scriptures, and that he appeared to Peter, and then to the twelve. (1 Corinthians 15:1–5)

> I am not ashamed of the gospel, because it is the power of God for the salvation of everyone who believes: first for the Jew then for the gentile. For in the gospel a righteousness from God is revealed, a righteousness that is by faith from first to last, just

as it is written: "The righteous will live by faith."
(Romans 1:16–17)

Believing the Word and believing the testimony of Jesus is paramount for salvation; otherwise we are calling God a liar. The gospel is the power of God for salvation and not baptism or good works. Baptism is a work done in the water, and the water is a witness to the revelation of Jesus Christ. It is believing over doubts of friends, family, and circumstances. We trust in God by faith over everything seen and unseen, whether it be legalism or someone's religious biases. It's, "I belong to God in Christ, and he belongs to me," and, "No, I'll never let go. And even if I should slip, he never will." For, "God who has called you into fellowship with his Son Jesus Christ is faithful" (1 Corinthians 1:9).

The apostle Paul wrote:

> For Christ did not send me to baptize, but to preach the gospel—not with words of human wisdom, less the cross be emptied of its power.
> For the message of the cross is foolishness to those who are perishing, but to us who are being saved it is the power of God. (1 Corinthians 1:17–18)

> For since in the wisdom of God the world through its wisdom did not know him, God "was pleased through the foolishness of what was preached to save those who believe." Jews demand miraculous signs and Greeks look for wisdom, but we preach Christ crucified: a stumbling block to Jews and foolishness to Gentiles, but to those whom God has called, both Jews and Greeks, Christ the power of God and the wisdom of God. (1 Corinthians 1:22–24)

Salvation is equally shared by all believers. Every believer is a unique child of God and an individual part of the body of Christ. Together we constitute the church of the living God, his family. Salvation has no degrees; there is no good, better, or best. In Christ we are all eternally saved from destruction. Eternal blessings are determined by one's obedience and service to Christ in this life, whereas salvation is by faith through grace. One's position in eternity is based on obedience, trust, what one did, and how he or she lived in the salvation given.

> So we make it our goal to please him, whether we are at home in the body or away from it. For we must all appear before the judgment seat of Christ, that each one may receive what is due him for the things done while in the body, whether good or bad. (2 Corinthians 5:9, 10)

Notice that the Word says "things done while in the body." The body of flesh is crucified with Christ. However, we, the new creation, will stand accountable before the Lord for the things that we were responsible for "while living in the body once we were saved." So it is an eternal decision to live in a way that pleases the Lord through obedience and good works through the power of the Spirit while magnifying the fruit of the Spirit as we live this life. We go through this life once. It would appear that the rewards, rebukes, punishments, or commendations would be given once, and that would be for our choices in this life.

> But we ought always to thank God for you, brothers loved by the Lord, "because from the beginning God chose you to be saved by the sanctifying work of the Spirit and through belief in the truth." He called you to this through our gospel, that you might share in the glory of our Lord Jesus Christ.

So then, brothers, stand firm and hold to the teachings we passed on to you, whether by word of mouth or by letter.

May our Lord Jesus Christ himself and God our Father, who loved us and by his grace gave us eternal encouragement and good hope, encourage your hearts and strengthen you in every good deed and word. (2 Thessalonians 2:13–17)

FAITH

WHERE IT COMES FROM,
WHAT COMES FROM IT

Consequently, faith comes from hearing the message,
and the message is heard through the word of Christ.
—Romans 10:17

And without faith it is impossible to please God,
because anyone who comes to him must believe that
he exists and that he rewards those who earnestly
seek him.

—Hebrews 11:6

SO FAITH COMES FROM HEARING and believing the gospel
message. It says we believe that God is truthful, reliable, powerful,
and totally deserving of our complete trust, and that he is able and
willing to do what he says he will do.

Again consider Abraham:

Against all hope, Abraham in hope believed and
so became the Father of many nations, just as it

had been said to him, "So shall your offspring be." Without weakening in his faith, he faced the fact that his body was as good as dead—since he was about a hundred years old—and that Sarah's womb was also dead. Yet he did not waver through unbelief regarding the promise of God, but was strengthened in his faith and gave glory to God, being fully persuaded that God had power to do what he had promised. "This is why it was credited to him as righteousness." (Romans 4:18–22)

The one who comes from above is above all; the one who is from the earth belongs to the earth, and speaks as one from the earth, The one who comes from heaven is above all. He testifies to what he has seen and heard, but no one accepts his testimony. The man who has accepted it has certified that God is truthful. (John 3:31–33)

Through him and for his name's sake, we have received grace and Apostleship to call people from among all the gentiles to the obedience that comes from faith. (Romans 1:5)

Therefore, since we have been justified through faith, we have peace with God through our Lord Jesus Christ, through whom we have gained access by faith into this grace in which we now stand. (Romans 5:1–2)

For we maintain that a man is justified by faith apart from the law. (Romans 3:28)

Since we have been justified by his blood, how much more shall we be saved from God's wrath through him. (Romans 5:9)

God presented him as a sacrifice of atonement, through faith in his blood. He did this to demonstrate his justice, because in his forbearance he had left the sins committed beforehand unpunished—he did this to demonstrate his justice at the present time, so as to be just and the one who justifies those who have faith in Jesus. (Romans 3:25–26)

But now a righteousness from God, apart from law, has been made known, to which the Law and the Prophets testify. This righteousness from God comes through faith in Jesus Christ to all who believe. (Romans 3:21–22)

What then shall we say? That the Gentiles, who did not pursue righteousness, have attained it, a righteousness that that is by faith; but Israel, who pursued a law of righteousness, has not obtained it. Why not? Because they pursued it not by faith but as if it were by works. (Romans 9:30–32)

He redeemed us in order that the blessing given to Abraham might come to the Gentiles through Christ Jesus, so that by faith we might receive the promise of the Spirit. (Galatians 3:14)

For it is by grace you have been saved, through faith—and this not from yourselves, it is the gift of God,—not by works, so that no one can boast. (Ephesians 2:8–9)

Let's take a look at this. Faith comes from hearing the message, his Word. *Faith* is an action word, and the action comes after hearing his Word. The message just may be that there is trouble coming, so take cover. And the response to the message by faith is taking cover. And why did you take cover? You believed the warning!

Faith makes it possible to please God. Obedience to God comes by faith. We are justified through faith and by faith. We gain access by faith into grace and are justified by faith in his blood. Righteousness from God comes through faith in Jesus Christ, which justifies those who have faith in Jesus. By faith we receive the promise of the Spirit, saved by grace through faith.

Faith, relying on our eternal God, has brought about victory after victory in the lives of the men of old as well as in recent times. Victory comes no matter the educational level of an individual or one's birth order; King David was the youngest of eight. No matter the country that one is born in, what family one is born into, or which religion one came out of, "He who has the Son has life, he who does not have the Son of God does not have life" (1 John 5:12). The question is, Do you believe the God of the Bible and call on him through Jesus?

We receive the entire package when we are saved. At that point we are washed in Jesus's blood, filled with his Spirit, made righteous, made holy, sealed, seated with Christ in heaven, given favor, given grace, made members of the body of Christ, forgiven, and spared from eternal judgment. Our names are written in the Lamb's Book of Life, and we receive new names. Then our responsibility becomes honoring God and living up to the high calling we have received, the honor he has placed on us by calling us his children.

We can see that faith and believing are keys to answered prayer in the kingdom of God. Someone may ask, "Well what is the difference between faith and belief?" Suppose someone called and said that he or she put a check for $1 million in your mailbox. You may thank the person because you have heard of this individual and believe him or her to be truthful. Yet unless you acted on what you believed to be true and by faith went to check your mailbox and retrieve the check, you would never have it. Believing is believing, and faith is acting on what you believe.

Suppose you are in your car (world), and there are many things to get done, situations to handle, people who need healing, and so on. You would like to get moving on one or all, so you put your key into the ignition and turn it on. The key is faith. You turn on the ignition, and there is ignition; the fire flows through the electrical system. The crank begins to turn, the pistons and valves are on the move, and the fuel pump is pushing gas through the injectors. The Holy Spirit is the fire flowing through the system, and prayer is the pump pushing the gas, which is the energy needed to power the engine. Then there is combustion, the explosion that drives the engine in perfect harmony as all the parts work together, coordinated, in perfect unity as each part does its work. Suddenly you're sitting behind a 1,000-horsepower mover. The air is working, as are all the lights, turn signals, the radio, heated and air-conditioned seats, and the steering wheel. Power seats, the backup camera, power mirrors, cruise control, power door locks, power windows, all-wheel drive, adjustable power suspension, GPS, and all the regulators and controls are working. The plugs, coils, thermostat, and running temperature are also working in the correct firing order and operation.

My point is this: So many individual parts laid out on the floor, all jumbled up, would look like an impossible task for most of us to figure out, put together, and get working. Even when families are in turmoil, relationships are misfiring, jobs and careers are a mess, and there is trouble on the right and the left, God is able to rearrange the parts and get our lives firing on all cylinders.

You turned the key of faith, and the Holy Spirit reacts and begins to work on your behalf in ways that no human can completely understand, working out even the smallest details. A situation may appear as one giant monster, yet the Lord is able to turn that monster into a 1,000-horsepower powerhouse designed to bless you. Be patient, and wait until he gets it together. There is one unfathomable intellect controlling all. He is an architect, an engineer, a builder, our Creator, a chemist, a mathematician, a biologist, a physicist, a metallurgist, a psychologist, and so much more. We could never comprehend the power, wisdom, and knowledge of God.

THE DAY OF SALVATION

GOD SAYS HIS SALVATION SHALL last forever. There are some who equate forever with a hair permanent: it's permanent until it falls apart. Too much humidity, and there goes that perm. Then you're off to the salon to get a new permanent. It's really not a perm but a temporary. Is God's salvation permanent or temporary? Does it fall apart like someone's hairdo?

Eternal life is as immutable as God is for it is of him and in him. He chose to give us new life, not an extension of the old one. There is no connection between the old and the new. One is carnal and one is spiritual; one is dead and the other alive. One is from the first Adam and the other from the second Adam, who is Jesus. One was created in dirt, and the other in life, the Spirit. Adam was created while Jesus did the creating.

Eternal life in Christ cannot be lost, misplaced, loaned, given up, walked away from, or traded for religion. One may even lose one's mind.

> Never the less, God's "solid" foundation "stands firm sealed with with this inscription: "The Lord knows those who are his", and, "Everyone who

confesses the name of the Lord must turn away from wickedness." (2 Timothy 2:19)

Someone may ask the question, "Well when does my salvation really kick in for keeps?"

> It still remains that some will enter that rest, and those who formerly had the gospel preached to them did not go in, because of their disobedience. Therefore God again set a certain day, calling it today, when a long time later he spoke through David, as was said before: "Today, if you here his voice, do not harden your hearts." (Hebrews 4:6–7)

So the time for salvation is now—right now. This is the day. It is time to call on the name of the Lord, and God says my salvation will last forever. Well, it is eternal from the moment we receive Jesus.

When did your life kick in? Was it when you turned twenty-one or when you were conceived? So when does one's eternal life kick in? At some magical time, or when we are born again?

There are scriptures that when twisted or used with limited understanding or investigation in conjunction with other scriptures can sound as is if a believer, one born of the Spirit, can lose what Christ Jesus died to give us—salvation. Through salvation, we are rescued from the wrath of God through the forgiveness of sins and renewal of the Holy Spirit, all of which came through Jesus Christ our Savior.

Ever heard this one, "Many will say to me on that day, Lord, Lord, did we not prophesy in your name, and in your name drive out demons and perform many miracles? Then I will them plainly, I never knew you. Away from me, you evil doers" (Matthew 7:22–24)?

This Word preached negatively and without understanding can and does produce fear and dread in the hearts of many Christians. However, this passage is actually speaking of religious nonbelievers, *not* the saints of God.

Let's look at the Matthew 7:21: "Not every one who says to me Lord, Lord, will enter the kingdom of heaven, but only he who does the will of my Father who is in heaven."

So let's put it together and investigate what's being left out. This passage is about salvation. According to verse 22, we must do the will of God to be saved. And what is that exactly? To be nice, to do good, and to go to church on Sunday? Sure, but those actions alone don't save anyone.

In John 6:37–40, the will of God for salvation is laid out plainly and concisely:

> All that the Father gives to me will come to me, and whoever comes to me I will never drive away. "I *will never drive away.*" For I have come down from heaven not to do my will but to do the will of him who sent me. "And this is the will of him who sent me," that I shall loose none of all that he has given me, but raise them up on the last day. "I *shall loose none.*" "For my Father's will is" that everyone who looks to the Son and believes in him shall have eternal life, and I will raise him up at the last day. I *will raise them up.* (emphasis added)

Notice that he does not ask your opinion or mine.

> "And by that will," we have been made holy through the sacrifice of the body of Jesus Christ once for all. (Hebrews 10:10)

This is the will of God for salvation, "to look to the Son and believe in him." Jesus spoke the words to the religious folks attempting to justify themselves by their works. They were saying, "Look at what we did," not, "Look at what you did for me on the cross." So he told them to depart because "I never knew you." Let's compare that statement to John 10:14–15: "I am the good shepherd; I know my sheep and they know me—just as the Father knows me and I know the Father—and I lay my life down for the sheep." Jesus said, "I know my sheep." And we're told in Matthew 7:22–24 they were not his for they had never put their faith in Jesus but did their own thing.

"The world and its desires pass away, but the man who does the will of God lives forever" (1 John 2:17). And the will of God is what? Looking to Jesus!

I have spoken to some who say, "Well, you can walk away." Exactly where are they going to go since God lives in us by his Spirit and fills all space and time? And he has told us, "Never will I leave you. Never will I forsake you." God did not say that you would not try and leave him. But he did say he will never leave you: "You are not your own; you were bought at a price" (1 Corinthians 6:19b, 20), and that price was his life. And if he bought you, he owns you. King David said in Psalm 139:8, "If I go to the heavens you are there; if I make my bed in the depths, you are there." The Lord said, *"And this is the will of him who sent me, that I shall lose none of all that he has given me."* (John 6:39) And Jesus also said, "You did not choose me, but I chose you and appointed you to go and bear fruit—fruit that will last. Then the Father will give you what ever you ask in my name" (John 15:16). He chose us to be saved through belief in the truth. Remember, we are not talking about this rebellious dirt that we live in but the new creation, the born-again believer created to be like God in true righteousness. The alien that lives within.

HOW DID WE GET THERE?

EVER THINK ABOUT EXACTLY HOW we came to know Jesus as our Lord and Savior? When many of us were doubters and rebelled greatly, we were totally worthless. Yet we ended up as saints, many even preaching the good news they railed against.

Well, Jesus tells us in John 6:37, "All that the Father gives to me will come to me, and who-ever comes to I will never drive away." So coming to Jesus is not accidental, as we shall see. Neither was it your idea nor mine. We were God the Father's creation, and he gave us to Jesus. We were given to Jesus for eternal life, adopted as his children, and given a place in his kingdom.

> Father I want those you have given me to be with me where I am, [with Jesus], and to see my glory, the glory you have given me because you loved me before the creation of the world. (John 17:24)

THE SAINTS

LET'S EXPLORE THIS BEGINNING AT our beginning.

> For you created my inmost being; you knit me together in my mother's womb. I praise you because I am fearfully and wonderfully made; your works are wonderful, I know that full well. My frame was not hidden from you when I was made in the secret place. When I was woven together in the depths of the earth, your eyes saw my unformed body. All the days ordained for me were written in your book before one of them came to be. (Psalm 139:13–16)

> O Lord you have searched me and you know me. 2 You know when I sit and when I rise; you perceive my thoughts from afar. 3 You discern my going out and my lying down; you are familiar with all my ways. Before a word is on my tongue you know it completely, O Lord. (Psalm 139:1–4)

Even though God knows us completely, because of his great love for us, he drew us to Jesus. He has a plan!

FOR THE WORD SAYS

For those God foreknew he also Predestined to be conformed to the likeness of his Son, that he might be the firstborn among many brothers. And those he Predestined, he also Called; those he Called, he also Justified; those he Justified, he also Glorified.

—Romans 8:29, 30

WE ARE NOT CREDITED WITH doing anything. God our Father, through Jesus, has done everything. We are complete in him.

To God's Elect, strangers in the world, scattered throughout Pontus, Galatia, Cappadocia, Asia, and Bithynia, "who have been Chosen" according to the Foreknowledge of God the Father, Through the Sanctifying Work of the Spirit, for Obedience to Jesus Christ and Sprinkling by his Blood. (1 Peter 1:1–3)

For he Chose us in him before the creation of the world to be holy and blameless in his sight. (Ephesians 1:4)

OUR COMING TO THE LORD JESUS CHRIST IS TOTALLY OF AND BY GOD

No one can come to me unless the Father who sent me draws him, and I will raise him up at the last day.

—John 6:44

He went on to say, "This is why I told you that no one can come to me unless the Father has enabled him.

—John 6:65

Do you not know that your body is a temple of the Holy Spirit, who is in you, whom you have received from God? You are not your own; you were bought at a Price. Therefore honor God with your body.

—1 Corinthians 6:19, 20

And we pray this in order that you may live a life worthy of the Lord and may please him in every way: bearing fruit in every good work, growing in the knowledge of God, being strengthened with all power according to his glorious might so that you may have great endurance and patience, and joyfully giving thanks to the Father, "who has "Qualified you" to share in the inheritance of the saints in the kingdom of light. For he has Rescued us from the dominion of darkness and brought into the kingdom of the Son he loves, in whom we have redemption, the forgiveness of sins.

—Colossians 1:10–14

I write to you, dear children, because your sins have been Forgiven on account of his name.

—1 John 2:12

MADE PERFECT

SPEAKING OF THE SAINTS OF old, "These were all commended for their faith, yet none of them received what had been promised. God had planned something better for us so that only together with us would they be made perfect" (Hebrews 11:39–40).

> Since that time he waits for his enemies to be made his foot stool, because by one sacrifice he has "Made Perfect Forever" those who are being made holy. (Hebrews 10:13–14)

Righteousness is a gift to all believers. Righteous isn't what we become by works. It's what we are, it's what we have been given, and it's what we have been made. The new birth, the new creation, is totally independent of the flesh. That is the carnal nature and the carnal mind. The sinful nature has no influence, adds nothing to eternal life, and cannot manipulate or control the Spirit of God. What the sinful nature can do is lead us into sin, compromise our testimonies, and make the lives of many around us, not to mention our own lives, miserable.

So I say live by the Spirit, and you will not gratify the desires of the sinful nature. For the sinful nature desires what is contrary to the Spirit, and the Spirit what is contrary to the sinful nature. They are in conflict with other, so that you do not do what you want. But if you are led by the Spirit, you are not under law.

The acts of the sinful nature are obvious: sexual immorality, impurity and debauchery; idolatry and witchcraft; hatred, discord, jealousy, fits of rage, selfish ambition, dissensions, factions and envy; drunkenness, orgies and the like. I warn you, as I did before, that those who live like this will not inherit the kingdom of God. (Galatians 5:16–21)

For if, by the trespass of the one man, death reigned through that one man, [Adam], how much more will those who receive God's abundant provision of grace and of the Gift of righteousness reign in life through the one man, Jesus Christ. (Romans 5:17)

And, if it is hard for the righteous to be saved, what will become of the ungodly and the sinner? (1 Peter 4:18)

WHAT DOES IT SAY?

> But grow in grace, and in the knowledge of our
> Lord and Savior Jesus Christ. To him be glory both
> now and forever! Amen.
>
> —2 Peter 3:18

THE WORD TELLS US TO grow in grace and in the knowledge of our Lord Jesus. If we are growing—and we are all growing—we haven't arrived yet. Some grow very fast while others grow very slowly. Some study the Word of God diligently and pray fervently, consistently, and expectantly. Others do not.

When you plant a seed, is its growth immediately detected? The roots of a new plant go down first into the soil, where the plant receives moisture, nourishment, and stability. If the plant or tree grew up toward the sky first, it probably wouldn't take long until it just fell over. And there are some people like that. They do not root into Christ. They just grow fast and tall, and then when testing comes they crash. Can we detect this plant while it is growing, establishing itself, and rooting in? Can we immediately detect the growth of a new believer?

Grow in grace. God gives all who come to him grace to grow.

Do we all have the same growing season? No. Do all people of God grow at the same rate, pace, depth of knowledge, and understanding? No. Just as children of any family have different personalities, likes, dislikes, quirks, assumptions, and priorities, so do the children of God. If we belong to Christ, our eternity, salvation, and the salvation of others are in him and totally independent of what you or I think about another's rate of growth, to say nothing of what we understand of our own growth. "I planted the seed, Apollos watered it, but God made it grow. So neither he who plants nor he who waters is anything, but only God who makes things grow" (1 Corinthians 3:6–7).

Yep, God does the growing.

> Salvation is found in no one else, for there is no other name under heaven given to men by which we must be saved. (Acts 4:12)

> Do not work for food that spoils, but for food that endures to eternal life, which the Son of Man will give you. On him God the Father has placed his seal of approval. Then they asked him. What must we do to do the works God requires? Jesus answered, "The work of God is this: to believe in the one he has sent." (John 6:27–29)

The Word says to grow in the grace and knowledge of our Lord and Savior Jesus Christ. If we are to grow in grace and knowledge of our Lord and Savior Jesus Christ, should we not have a workable understanding of the salvation that he died to give to us? Should we not have the depth and clarity to comprehend why eternal life is eternal from the moment it is received? The confidence and assurance results in inner peace. Verse 29 declares that believing in Jesus is the complete work that God requires for salvation.

> For God so loved the world that he gave his one and only son, that whoever believes in him shall not perish but have eternal life. For God did not send his son into the world to condemn the world, but save the world through him. "Whoever believes in him is not condemned," but whoever does not believe stands condemned already because he has not believed in the name of God's one and only son. (John 3:16–18)

Salvation is based on one thing, and that is believing in Jesus.

> But what does it say? "The word is near you; it is in your mouth and in your heart," that is, the word of faith we are proclaiming: That if you confess with your mouth, "Jesus is Lord," and believe in your heart that God has raised him from the dead, you will be saved. For it is with your heart that you believe and are justified, and it is with your mouth that you confess and are saved. As the Scripture says, "Anyone who trusts in him will never be put to shame." For there is no difference between Jew and Gentile-the same Lord is Lord of all and richly blesses all who call on him, for, "Everyone who calls on the name of the Lord will be saved." (Romans 10:8–13)

Notice there are no ifs, ands, or buts.

The Word, the message, the gospel is what we are believing, the testimony of Jesus, the Son of God, and what he has done for us. For at the very second we truly believe and call on his name, we are indwelled by the Holy Spirit who seals us to himself.

Confessing with our mouths, believing in our hearts, and calling on the Lord undoubtedly save us. But how? What exactly happens that guarantees us eternal life when we still fail, fall, sin, and at times act as if we've never even heard of the Lord Jesus Christ? We throw tantrums. We eye our neighbor's goods, wife, or husband and chase him or her when given half a chance. And at times we do some activities that are much worse than that. Eternal life is not something earned in any way but something received! Yes, it is a gift. "For the wages of sin is death, but the gift of God is eternal life in Christ Jesus our Lord" (Romans 6:23). The Word also says in Romans 11:29b, "God's gifts and his call are irrevocable."

The Greek word that has been translated as "irrevocable" in the New International Version and as "without repentance" in the King James Version is *ametameloma*. This Greek word means "not changing one's mind." In other words, God is not going to change his mind concerning the gift of eternal life that he has freely given to you or me (unchangeable, unalterable, and immovable). And eternal life is one of those gifts. A gift freely given, not earned or paid for by the one receiving the gift but by the one giving it. Got that? Paid for by the one giving the gift. Jesus bought this gift for us with his life! And there is nothing that we have to do to keep it because this gift was not given to us as some earthly gift that sits nicely on some table or mantle. Nor do we wear it as a sweater. Rather, this gift indwells our very beings. We are eternal children of God. Our very beings were changed from temporal to eternal. We are a new creation.

> For it is by grace you have saved, through faith—
> "and this not from yourselves," it is the gift of
> God—Not by works, so that no one can boast.
> (Ephesians 2:8–9)

The Holy Spirit is another irrevocable gift.

> If you love me, you will obey what I command. And
> I will ask the Father, and he will give you another
> "Counselor to be with you forever—" the Spirit of

truth. The world cannot accept him, because it neither sees him nor knows him. But you know him, for he lives with you and will be in you. (John 14:15–17)

Peter replied, "Repent and be baptized, everyone of you, in the name of Jesus Christ for the forgiveness of sins. And you will receive the gift of the Holy Spirit. The promise is for you and for your children and all who are far off-for all whom the Lord our God will call" (Acts 2:38–39).

But then the Word continues with, "Those who accepted his message were baptized, and about three thousand were added to their number that day" (Acts 2:41).

What was the message, the gospel message, and why did they accept it? Because they believed it; those being baptized were believers. And all believers receive the Holy Spirit when they believe and are sealed, whether or not they have been baptized.

If you then, though you are evil, know how to give good gifts to your children, how much more will your Father in heaven give the Holy Spirit to those who ask him. (Luke 11:13)

He redeemed us in order that the blessing given to Abraham might come to the Gentiles through Christ Jesus, so by faith we might receive the promise of the Spirit. (Galatians 1:14)

And you also were included in Christ when you heard the word of truth, the gospel of your salvation. "Having believed, you were marked in him with a seal, the promised Holy Spirit," who is a deposit guaranteeing our inheritance until the redemption of those who are God's possession-to the praise of his glory. (Ephesians 1:13–14)

Being water baptized in itself does not guarantee anyone the Holy Spirit unless he or she believes, and if one believes that person will receive the Holy Spirit regardless. And if someone does not believe when baptized, the guarantee is that he or she will get wet.

There are undoubtedly many gifts and promises given to believers in Christ. Let's deal with a few of those that pertain to eternal life.

Acts 2:38—Gift of the Holy Spirit
Romans 5:17—Gift of righteousness
Romans 6:23—Gift of God is eternal life through Christ Jesus
1 Peter 3:7—Gift of life
1 Corinthians 12:9—Faith

And I will ask the Father, and he will give you another counselor to be with you forever—the Spirit of truth. The world cannot accept him, because it neither sees him nor knows him. But you know him for he lives with you and will be in you. (John 14:16–17)

THE OLD TESTAMENT LAW

WHEN A BORN-AGAIN BELIEVER BREAKS the Ten Commandments, or any of them, does this cost the person his or her salvation? No. If it did, no one would be saved.

Though the biblical law is still viable and quite enforceable by God, it has no power over a believer for either eternal life or death. However, the Lord will use the law to judge the world of unbelievers.

There is a great distance between a believer and a nonbeliever. First of all, the believer is a child of God. Now, someone may ask, "Is not everyone a child of God? Are not all of us God's children?" No, we are all his creation but not all his children. All people are born of the flesh, fashioned out of the dust of the earth. But God's children have been born again, that is, born of the Spirit, whereby God has adopted them into his family and kingdom.

> And you have forgotten the word encouragement that addresses you as sons: "My son do not make light of the Lord's discipline, and do not loose heart when he rebukes you because the Lord disciplines those he loves, and he punishes everyone he accepts as a son." Endure hardship as discipline; God is

treating you as sons. For what son is not disciplined
by his father? (Hebrews 12:5–7)

So the unbeliever is condemned while the believer is punished.
Now the Word says that God punishes everyone that he accepts.
He knew in advance that most of us would need a redirection. God
knew your entire history, both before you were saved and after.
Before he accepted us, God knew what he was getting. And praise
God, he has a plan for the biggest sinner as well as the humblest.
Remember that old song, "What can wash away my sin? Nothing
but the blood of Jesus."

If anyone's name was not found written in the
book of life, he was thrown into the lake of fire.
(Revelation 20:15)

Do not think that I have come to abolish the Law
or the Prophets; I have not come to abolish them
but to fulfill them. I tell you the truth, until heaven
and earth disappear, not the smallest letter, nor
least stroke of a pen, will by any means disappear
from the Law until everything is accomplished.
Anyone who breaks one of the least of these
commandments and teachers others to do the same
will be called least in the kingdom of heaven, but
whoever practices and teaches these commands
will be called great in the kingdom of heaven.
(Matthew 5:17–19)

The law did not move or disappear. No part of the law will be
abolished until all is accomplished. So if the law hasn't changed,
what has? Us. We have moved from under the power of the law
because we died to it, and the law has no hold on the dead. "So, my
brothers, you also died to the Law through the body of Christ, that

you might belong to another, to Him who was raised from the dead, in order that we might bear fruit to God" (Romans 7:4).

Jesus, speaking about the law, says, whoever breaks it and teaches others to do that will be called least in the Kingdom of Heaven, but whoever shall do and teach them the same will be called great in the kingdom of heaven. This refers to believers, not unbelievers, there will be no unbelievers in heaven. So there are believers doing and teaching things that they should not.

Both are in heaven. Some were teaching the right things, and some were not. The differences are rewards and the stations we may occupy. What do you and I want to be called, least or great?

> For he himself is our peace, who has made the two one (Jews and gentiles, one people in Christ, all who are not Jews are gentiles) and has destroyed the barrier, the dividing wall of hostility, By *abolishing in his flesh the law* with its commandments and regulations. (Ephesians 2:14–15)

"Through Him everyone who believes is justified from everything you could not be justified from by the law of Moses" (Acts 13:39). He died for you and for me. He died in our place. The abolishing in his flesh set us free from the law of Moses. The law is abolished for every believer for it has been fulfilled for every believer.

> "Christ is the end of the law so that there may be righteousness for everyone that believes." (John 10:4)

You did not fulfill it for yourself; that is never sin. And I did not fulfill it for myself. Jesus did. Jesus was born God, the Son of God, as a man, being in his very nature God. We are born with a fallen Adamic nature. Not so for Jesus. We are born sinners and just go on sinning. Jesus was born sinless and never sinned. He was tempted just as we are, yet he was without sin. On that note, God accepted his sinless, selfless sacrifice on behalf of all those who would believe that message and put their trust in him. Neither you nor I can add to or subtract from something that is completed, finished, and settled.

And since God counts the work of salvation finished for you and me, we cannot change it, no matter what. Nothing can be added to it or subtracted from it. God said it is finished. That's with its commandments and regulations.

In the story about Lazarus and the rich man in the gospel of Luke, the rich man tried to have Lazarus sent to him from Abraham with a little water for he was in a place of torment. And what did Abraham say? "And besides all this, between us and you a great chasm has been fixed, so that those who want to go from here to you cannot, nor can anyone cross over from there to us" (Luke 16:26).

The final decision on receiving or rejecting the Lord Jesus before one departs this life is eternally binding. There is no crossing over, no water breaks, and no coming back. Nor will you be sent back once saved.

> Later, knowing that all was now completed, and so the scripture would be fulfilled, "Jesus said, I am thirsty." A jar of wine vinegar was there, so they soaked a sponge in it, put the sponge on a stalk of the hyssop plant, and lifted it to Jesus lips. When he had received the drink, Jesus said, "It is finished." With that, he bowed his head and gave up his spirit. (John 19:28–30)

> Now we know that whatever the law says, it says to those who are under the law, so that every mouth may be silenced, and the whole world held accountable God. Therefore no one will be declared righteous in his sight by observing the law; rather through the law we become conscious of sin. (Romans 3:19–20)

Praise God! We who belong to Christ are not under the law of sin and death. Whatsoever it says, it says to those who are under the law. That would be the unbeliever, those religious or nonreligious, those who refuse to believe, those who live by the works of the law, those with good intentions, or those who make no effort to serve the Lord in any way. In that case, the Word says to those depending on works, "Not good enough."

> We who are Jews by birth and not Gentile sinners' know that a man is not justified by observing the law, but by faith of Jesus Christ. So we too, have put our faith in Christ Jesus, that we may be justified by faith in Christ, and not by observing the law, because by observing the law no one will be justified. (Galatians 2:15–16)

There is not one law but two: the law of death and the law of life. When we give our hearts to Jesus and receive him as our Lord and Savior, we move from one to the other. "Therefore, there now no condemnation for those who are in Christ Jesus, because through Christ Jesus the law of the Spirit of life set me free from the law of sin and death" (Romans 8:1–2)

The law of the spirit of life sets us free from being condemned. Many preachers use this from feeling condemned, feelings have nothing to do with salvation. If we belong to Jesus, we cannot be condemned. For God only gave us one new law, and that would be the law of life. So the Old Testament law is the law of Moses, the law of sin and death. The New Testament law is the law of the spirit, the law of life. There is nothing greater; nothing will change, cancel, or overpower the spirit of life. Nothing can nullify the salvation of a born again believer.

We are all born under the law of sin and death from our first breath to the very moment that we call on Jesus for forgiveness and salvation. Christ Jesus has made us free from the law of sin and death.

"Christ is the end of the law so that there may be righteousness for everyone who believes" (Romans 10:4).

Christ is the end of the law because he fulfilled it on behalf of every believer by living his life under the law and dying having never transgressed. So his life was sinless. And now that the law is fulfilled for every believer, we are deemed righteous, "without blemish and free from accusation" (Colossians 1:22b).

> Where, O death, is your victory? Where, O death, is your sting?
>
> The sting of death is sin, and the power of sin is the law. But thanks be to God! He gives us the victory through our Lord Jesus Christ. (1 Corinthians 15:55–56)

Death has no sting. In Christ as the grave has no victory, there is no eternal death in Christ. Nor is the grave our eternal home. Sin is the cause of death for all humankind. It gets its strength or power from the law. So guess what? If there is no law, sin has no power.

> And where there is no law there is no transgression. (Romans 4:15b)

> But sin is not taken into account when there is no law. (Romans 5:15b)

> For sin shall not be your master, because you are not under law, but under grace. (Romans 6:14)

AND TO THE GENTILES, NO LAW

All who sin apart from the law will also perish apart from the law, and all who sin under the law will be judged by the law. For it is not those who hear the law who are righteous in God's sight, but it is those who obey the law who will be declared righteous. (Indeed, when the "gentiles, who do not have the law," do by nature things required by the law, they are a law for themselves, even though they do not have the law, since they show that the requirements of the law are written on their hearts, their consciences also bearing witness, and their thoughts now accusing, now even defending them.)

—Romans 2:12–15

He has revealed his word to Jacob, his laws and decrees to Israel. He has done this for no other nation; they do not know his laws.

—Psalm 147:19–20

The Gentiles are not now, nor were they ever, under the Mosaic law for it was only given to Israel and no other nation. It was God's covenant with them.

> Then the Lord said to Moses, "Write down these words, for in accordance with these words I have made a covenant with you and Israel." Moses was there with the Lord forty days and forty nights without eating bread or drinking water. And he wrote on the tablets the words of the covenant—the ten commandments. (Exodus 34:27–28)

> Hear the word the Lord spoken against you, O people of Israel-against the whole family I brought up out of Egypt: "You only have I chosen of all the families of the earth; therefore I will punish you for all your sins." (Amos 3:1–2)

> For I could wish that I myself were cursed and cut off from Christ for the sake of my brothers, those of my own race, the people of Israel. Theirs is the adoption as sons; theirs the divine glory, the covenants, the receiving of the law, the temple worship and the promises. Theirs are the patriarchs, and from them is traced the human ancestry of Christ, who is God over all, forever praise! Amen. (Romans 9:3–5)

Though the law was given to Israel, it was essential for the salvation of the world:

> Before this faith came, we were held prisoners by the law, locked up until faith should be revealed. "So the law was put in charge to lead us to Christ" that we might be justified by faith. Now that faith

has come, we are no longer under the supervision of the law. (Galatians 3:23–25)

What shall we say, then? Is the law sin? Certainly not! Indeed I would not have known what sin was except through the law. For I would not have known what coveting really was if the law had not said, "Do not covet." But sin, seizing the opportunity afforded by the commandment, produced in me every kind of covetous desire. For apart from the law sin is dead. Once I was alive apart from the law; but when the commandment came, sin sprang to life and I died. I found that the very commandment that was intended to bring life actually brought death. (Romans 7:7–10)

The law revealed sin to the world and the penalty for breaking it. There was no way out from under it or the eternal consequences of breaking it. But the Word says where there is no law there is no sin, because sin is not taken into account when there is no law.

Suppose you're driving along at 140 miles an hour and get pulled over by the police. They say that you were driving too fast, and they would like to give you a summons. However, there are no posted speed limit signs anywhere for there has never been a law concerning speed. So, if there are no laws, you can do pretty much what you want and not worry about it.

Now if a sign appeared the next day and said that the speed limit was fifty-five and the penalty for driving fifty-six was death, your attitude would probably change pretty quickly. If you got caught driving fifty-six, and your neck was on the line, you would be looking for a way out. Jesus is the way out.

God was going to send his Son, Jesus, the Savior of the world. But if the world did not know what God's laws were and the penalty for breaking them, why would they see a reason to embrace a Savior, not knowing they needed one?

Now with God's laws posted, we understand that we are a bunch of lawbreakers in need of someone to save us from the penalty. For we are without excuses. And we still want to drive 140 miles an hour.

So the Old Testament law was put in charge to reveal what sin is and to lead us to Christ.

THE COMMAND

WHEN THE LAW WAS GIVEN, we were already dead, and the law had no power to reverse it. Yet the law didn't kill us. But breaking one commandment in Genesis did.

> And the Lord God commanded the man, "You are free to eat from any tree in the garden; but you must not eat from the tree of the knowledge of good and evil, for when you eat of it you will surely die."
> (Genesis 2:16–17)

We know the story. Eve ate and offered Adam a bite of the fruit. It looked good, so he tried it and humanity died. No matter how good or bad something looks or sounds, the truth is in the Word of God. The final result of every situation will be exactly what he says it will be. Disobedience destroys, and in this case, it killed all humankind. Disobedience not only affects the disobedient but can affect all those who are connected with him.

> Therefore, just as sin entered the world through one man, and death through sin, and in this way death came to all men, because all sinned—for before

> the law was given, sin was in the world. But sin
> is not taken into account when there is no law.
> Nevertheless, death reigned from the time of Adam
> to the time of Moses, even over those who did not
> sin by breaking a command, as did Adam, who was
> a pattern of the one to come. (Romans 5:12–14)

Yes, Adam and Eve died spiritually, and physical death was also passed on to all humankind, so they began producing, after their kind, dead copies. Adam was the pattern, the first. If the first copy is flawed, then every subsequent copy from the same mold will have the same flaw until another flawless original is introduced in the place of the first run, making the first run obsolete.

The breaking of the commandment produced death in every individual ever born but one, Jesus, the flawless original, the first new creation. God became flesh while we, flesh, became born of the Spirit, filled with the Spirit, and the children of God.

The first man, Adam, was fashioned from the natural elements, dust. Eve was fashioned from a rib. Where did that dust come from? Was it lying on the earth and that the earth was relatively new? Maybe. So that dust may have been from creation. Since Adam was created from that dust, he was probably comprised of a little bit of every natural element in the universe.

> All of us also lived among them at one time,
> gratifying the cravings of our sinful nature and
> following its desires and thoughts. Like the rest we
> were by nature objects of wrath. (Ephesians 2:3)

> Whoever believes in the Son has eternal life, but
> whoever rejects the Son will not see life for God's
> wrath remains on him. (John 3:36)

The fallen man, by his very nature, is sinful and subject to God's continual wrath because humanity continually sins. No person can change his or her nature. Nor will that nature be redeemed.

> If there is a natural body, there is also a spiritual body. So it is written: "The first man Adam became a living being" the last Adam, a life giving Spirit. The spiritual did not come first, but the natural, and after that the spiritual. The first man was of the dust of the earth, the second man from heaven. As was the earthly man, so are those who are of the earth; and as is the man from heaven, so also are those who are of heaven. And just as we have borne the likeness of the earthly man, so shall we bear the likeness of the man from heaven. (1 Corinthians 15:44b–49)

> Since then, you have been raised with Christ, set your hearts on things above, where Christ is seated at the right hand of God. Set your minds on things above, not on earthly things. For you died, and your life is now hidden with Christ in God. When Christ, who is your life, appears, then you also will appear with him in glory. (Colossians 3:1–4)

First, the apostle Paul tells us that we are risen with Christ, if indeed we belong to him, and to seek heavenly things where Christ is seated. Set your affection or heart on those things that are above and not on earthly things. Why? Because you're dead. Not physically dead, but dead to those things in this creation, carnal or natural. Now you're in Christ, a new creation, created in Christ Jesus, eternal, for we are alive to and in Christ. And because you and I are dead to this creation, our lives are hidden with Christ in God. So when Christ, who is one's life, shall appear, then you and I shall also appear with him in glory.

DEAD TO WHAT?

DEAD TO DEATH, VERSES 8–11

What shall we say, then? Shall we go on sinning so that grace may increase? By no means! We died to sin; how can we live in it any longer? Or don't you know that all of us who were baptized into Christ Jesus were baptized into his death? We were therefore buried with him through baptism into death in order that, just as Christ was raised from the dead through the glory of the Father, we to may live a new life.

If we have been united with him like this in his death, we will certainly also be united with him in his resurrection. For we know that our old self was crucified with him so that the body of sin might be done away with, that we should no longer be slaves to sin—because anyone who has died has been freed from sin.

Now if we died with Christ, we believe that we shall also live with him. For we know that since Christ was raised from the dead, he cannot die again; "death no longer has mastery over him." The death he died, he died to sin once for all; but the life he lives, he lives to God.

"In the same way, count yourselves dead to sin but alive to God in Christ Jesus." Therefore do not let sin reign in your mortal bodies so that you obey its evil desires. (Romans 6:1–12)

That's where repentance comes in. The Word says to turn away from sin and not let it reign. Avoid fornication, adultery, drunkenness, lying, stealing, untrustworthiness, unfaithfulness, undependability, and whatever else fits.

For as in Adam all die, so in Christ all will be made alive. (1 Corinthians 15:22)

MADE ALIVE

(QUICKENED)

> When you were dead in your sins and in the uncircumcision of your sinful nature, God made you alive with Christ. He forgave all our sins, having canceled the written code, with its regulations, that was against us and stood opposed to us; he took it away, nailing it to the cross. And having disarmed the powers and authorities, he made a public spectacle of them, triumphing over them by the cross.
>
> —Colossians 2:13–15

As for you, you were dead in your transgressions and sins, in which you used to live when you followed the ways of this world and of the ruler of the kingdom of the air, the spirit who is at work in those who are disobedient. All of us also lived among them at one time, gratifying the cravings of our sinful nature and following its desires and thoughts. Like the rest we were by nature objects of wrath. But because of his great love for us, God, who is rich in mercy, made us alive with Christ even when we were dead in transgressions-it is by grace you have been saved. "And God raised us up with Christ and seated us with him in the heavenly realms in Christ Jesus," in order that in the coming ages he might show the incomparable riches of his grace, expressed in his kindness to us in Christ Jesus.

—Ephesians 2:1–7

WHEN WE WERE DEAD IN our sins, God made us alive through Jesus, having forgiven all our sins and trespasses. Being made eternally alive is not a process; it's an irreversible one-time event. He blotted out the law that was against us, removed it from us, and nailed it to the cross. The power of sin being in the law no longer has power over a believer and disarms satanic forces that would use it to keep us bound.

I tell you the truth, whoever hears my word and believes him who sent me has eternal life and will not be condemned; he has crossed over from death to life. (John 5:24)

"We have this hope as an anchor for the soul, firm and secure." It enters the inner sanctuary behind the curtain, where Jesus, who went before us, has entered on our behalf. He has become a high priest forever, in the order of Melchizedek. (Hebrews 6:19–20)

May God himself, the God of peace, sanctify you through and through. May your whole spirit, soul and body be kept blameless at the coming of our Lord Jesus Christ. "The one who calls you is faithful and he will do it." (1 Thessalonians 5:23–24)

Not condemned but passed from one reality to another, from an eternity of damnation to one of eternal life. Notice that it does not say moving toward it, or never sin again, or it will be canceled or reconsidered.

No, eternal life is not an external garment that can be put on and removed. It is now who we are, eternal people. We have been changed, given a new nature, and changed into a new creation. We have no part of the old one; the old has no hold on us. That is one's spiritually renewed new person.

But we still battle the flesh, in the flesh, until the our bodies are redeemed. And we battle the forces of darkness, evil in high places. If we have come to know Jesus as our Lord and Savior, the battle is not for our salvation but our faith, which Satan works continually to destroy. And so we battle and pray for the salvation of others. And that battle is relentless, whether or not we understand and acknowledge it.

> At one time we too were foolish, disobedient, deceived and enslaved by all kinds and pleasures. We lived in malice and envy, being hated and hating one another. But when the kindness and love God of our savior appeared, he saved us, not because of righteous things we had done, but because of his mercy. He saved us through the washing of rebirth and renewal by the Holy Spirit, whom he poured out on us generously through Jesus Christ our Savior, so that having been justified by his grace, we might become heirs having the hope of eternal life. (Titus 3:3–7)

The apostle begins by telling us in verse 3 how sinful and disobedient we were. But when the love and kindness of God, our Savior, appeared, he saved us, not because of anything that we had done but because of his mercy. He saved us by the washing of regeneration and renewing by the Holy Spirit. He did not save us because we helped someone cross the street or did any other good deed for none of those things could do what needed to be done; that is, change us.

Saved us—past tense, done deal. And how did the Lord accomplish that? By the new birth; believing in his name and calling on him in faith through which righteousness comes. And by being made alive by the Holy Spirit—that is, being born again—born of the Spirit and renewed by the Holy Spirit, which God our Father does sovereignly.

> Moreover, we have all had human fathers who disciplined us and we respected them for it. How much more should we submit to the Father of our spirits and live. (Hebrews 12:9)

If we believe that the Father of our spirit, which is the new creation, is perfect, what does that make us? The Word says that we were created to be like God in true righteousness and holiness. It also says, "Because by one sacrifice he has made perfect forever those who are being made holy" (Hebrews 10:14).

So our eternal Father is God himself. It is not that we become children of God magically or grow into the position by good works. No, we are born-again children through the new birth.

> If there is a natural body, there is a spiritual body. So it is written: "The first man Adam became a living being," the last Adam, a life-giving spirit. The spiritual did not come first, but the natural, and after that the spiritual. The first man was of the dust of the earth, the second man from heaven. As was the earthly man, so are those who are of the earth; and is the man from heaven, so also are those who are of heaven. And just as we have borne the likeness

of the earthly man, so shall we bear the likeness of
the man from heaven. (1 Corinthians 15:44b–49)

Let us look at the natural and relate it to the Spirit. It's like this:
Mother and Dad get married, and after a while, Mom is found to
be with child. It takes two. Mother had an egg, but by itself, it is
for all intents and purposes dead until it is invaded and occupied
by Dad. And then, miraculously, life begins. This new life does not
need to grow to some point in the future when it suddenly becomes
the offspring of these parents. No, this new life is their child at the
moment of conception and continues to grow through its life in the
womb and out as their child.

Now suppose pregnant mom robs a bank, kills a teller, and
then burns the bank down. Can you hold the baby within her
womb responsible? Are you able to make the case that baby was an
accomplice, ringleader, or willing participant? Of course not. Even
though baby was present at every event, baby is totally innocent. The
old—that is, the mommy—suffers the consequences. The new—
that is, the baby (new birth)—does not.

Though baby is in this person, this baby is not this person for the
baby has a different DNA signature. This baby is neither the mommy
nor the daddy. No, the baby is a new creation with both his or her
mother's and father's signatures. But the baby has a life and identity
all his or her own. Now the baby naturally is created in likeness after
his or her human dad—not the spiritual Father but the carnal; not
the eternal but the temporal, after the original Adam.

However, when Jesus enters a person through the Holy Spirit
and enters the dead spirit of a person, there is life, looking at it from
the natural, and suddenly, this person becomes a child of God.
God now becomes this person's dad since this person is *born* of the
Spirit. And because this born-again person has God himself as his
or her eternal Dad, like the eternal Dad, this person is also eternal.
This person has been given new birth into an everlasting family and
kingdom. Yes, this person is truly a new creation.

The flesh, the mind of a human, and who or what the carnal person was has no bearing on the child of God, who is the stranger and alien within.

An old man was crucified with Christ: "I have been crucified with Christ and I no longer live, but Christ lives in me. The life I live in the body, I live by faith in the Son of God, who loved me and gave himself for me" (Galatians 2:20).

NOT A RELIGIOUS EVENT
OR HUMAN DEED

I want you to know how much I am struggling for you and for those at Laodicea, and for all who have not met personally. My purpose is that they may be encouraged in heart and united in love, so that they may have the full riches of complete understanding, in order that they may know the mystery of God, namely Christ, in whom are hidden all the treasures of wisdom and knowledge. I tell you this so that no one may deceive you by fine-sounding arguments. For though I am absent from you in body, I am present with you in spirit and delight to see how orderly you are and how firm your faith in Christ is.

So then, just as you received Christ Jesus as Lord, continue to live in him, rooted and built up in him, strengthened in the faith as you were taught and overflowing with thankfulness.

See to it that no one takes you captive through hollow and deceptive philosophy, which depends on human tradition and the basic principles of the world rather than on Christ.

For in Christ all the fullness of the Deity lives in bodily form, and you have been given fullness in Christ, who is the head over every power and authority.

In him you were also circumcised, in putting off the sinful nature, not with a circumcision done by the hands of men but with a circumcision done by Christ, having been buried with him in baptism and raised with through your faith in the power of God, who raised him from the dead.

When you were dead in your sins and in the uncircumcision of your sinful nature, God made you alive with Christ. He forgave us all our sins, having canceled the written code, with its regulations, that was against us qnd stood opposed to us; he took it away, nailing it to the cross. And having disarmed the powers and authorities, he made a public spectacle of them, triumphing over them by the cross.

Therefore do not let anyone judge you by what you eat or drink, or with regard to a religious festival, a New Moon, celebration or a sabbath day. These are a shadow of the things that were to come; the reality, however, is found in Christ. Do not let anyone who delights in false humility and the worship of angels disqualify you for the prize. Such a person goes into great detail about what he has seen and his unspiritual mind puffs him up with idle notions. He has lost connection with the Head, from whom the whole body, supported and held together by its ligaments and sinews, grows as God causes it to grow.

> "Since you died with Christ to the basic principles of the world, why," as though you still belonged to it, do you submit to its rules: Do not handle! Do not taste! Do not touch!" These are all destined to perish with use, because they are based on human commands and teachings. Such regulations indeed have an appearance of wisdom, with their self-imposed worship, their false humility and their harsh treatment of the body, but they lack any value in restraining sensual indulgence.
>
> —Colossians 2:1–23

VERSE 10 TELLS US WE have fullness in Christ. Nothing can add to that completeness. Our perfection in the Lord Jesus is beyond the bounds of creation. Anything else is only a shadow, whether it be false humility, sacrificial food or drink, or a sabbath day, holy day, or any other day. The shadow has no control over eternity. The shadow has no light, no substance, no longevity, no depth, and no power.

THE BLOOD

For the life of a creature is in the blood, and I have given it to you to make atonement for yourselves on the alter; it is the blood that makes atonement for one's life.

—Leviticus 17:11

THE BLOOD IS THE LIFE, and the life is in the blood. The blood travels to every part of the body, carrying with it life—that is, oxygen—and removing impurities. If the heart ceases to pump, the blood stops moving. The body has only a few minutes to live as the brain and every cell are starved of oxygen. The heart pumps life!

But now a righteousness from God, apart from law, has been made known, to which the Law and the Prophets testify. "This righteousness from God comes through faith in Jesus Christ to all who believe." There is no difference, for all have sinned and fall short of the glory of God, and are justified freely by his grace through the redemption that came by Christ Jesus. God presented him as a sacrifice of atonement, through faith in his blood.

He did this to demonstrate his justice, because
in his forbearance he had left the sins committed
beforehand unpunished-he did it to demonstrate
his justice at the present time, "so as to be just and
the one who justifies those who have faith in Jesus."
(Romans 3:21–26)

Verse 25 reads, "Through faith in his blood." As we learned
earlier in the book, *faith* is an action word. So the action is
responding to the message that has been preached. First John 1:7b
tells us, "And the blood of Jesus, his Son, purifies us from all sin."
That means believing that Jesus is the Son of God and that he died
for sins—yours and mine—and was raised from the dead. If we
believe that, then the faith expressed is asking Jesus in prayer to be
our personal Savior by calling on his name for life. Some call that
the Sinner's Prayer.

For he has rescued us from the dominion of darkness
and brought us into the kingdom of the Son he
loves, in whom we have redemption, the forgiveness
of sins. (Colossians 1:13–14)

For God was pleased to have all his fullness dwell
in him, and through him to reconcile to himself all
things, whether things on earth or things in heaven,
by making peace through his blood, shed on the
cross. (Colossians 1:19–20)

Salvation is given to each person who by faith receives Jesus. The
completed work of God is the result of every aspect of the gospel
working together.

If Jesus had not died for our sins, then they would not be paid
for. If the blood of Jesus had not cleansed us of our sins, there would
be no forgiveness. If the Holy Spirit had not been poured out, there

would be no salvation. If God the Father had not accepted the sacrifice of Jesus by raising him from the dead, there would be no justification or resurrection.

There are some who believe salvation without the work of the Holy Spirit is possible. Since you are cleansed by the blood and forgiven, that's all you need.

> You, however, are controlled not by the sinful nature but by the Spirit, if the Spirit of God lives in you, "And if anyone does not have the Spirit of Christ he does not belong to Christ." But if Christ is in you, your body is dead because of sin, yet your spirit is alive because of righteousness. And if the Spirit of him who raised Jesus from the dead is living in you, He who raised Christ from the dead will also give life to your mortal bodies through His Spirit, who lives in you. (Romans 8:9–11)

> "The Spirit gives life, the flesh counts for nothing." The words I have spoken to you are Spirit and they are life. (John 6:63)

Well, let's think about it for a minute. Each work of salvation opens the way for the next. The Lord Jesus said that unless a person is born again, he or she cannot see or enter the kingdom of God. The new birth isn't accomplished by the blood but by the Spirit because the washing in the blood, which is also done by the Holy Spirit, opens the way for the Holy Spirit to do his work. The Holy Spirit only lives in clean, washed vessels, and the only cleanser powerful enough to clean a believer is the blood of Jesus Christ.

A person can be forgiven, but that does not guarantee the person is changed. Someone may say, "I forgive you," but that does nothing unless there is an inner transformation. The only one who transforms a sinner into a saint worthy of being adopted into the family of God is God. And the sinner transformed into a saint and indwelled by God because he or she has been forgiven.

Forgiveness comes from believing.

> He commanded us to preach to the people and to testify that he is the one whom God appointed as judge of the living and the dead. all the prophets testify about him that everyone that believes in him, [Jesus], receives forgiveness of sins through his name.
>
> While Peter was still speaking these words, the Holy Spirit came on all who heard the message. (Acts 10:42–44)

Do you understand the sequence of events? The message preached; that is, the gospel. From the believing of the message comes immediate forgiveness followed by an immediate outflowing of the Holy Spirit. "Those controlled by the sinful nature cannot please God" (Romans 8:8).

BORN AGAIN

Now there was a man of the Pharisees named Nicodemus a member of the Jewish council. He came to Jesus at night and said, Rabbi we know you are a teacher who has come from God. For no one could perform the miraculous signs you are doing if God were not with him.

In reply Jesus declared, 'I tell you the truth, no one can see the kingdom of God unless he is born again."

"How can a man be born when he is old?" Nicodemus asked, "Surely he cannot enter a second time into his mother's womb to be born!"

Jesus answered, "I tell you the truth, no one can enter the kingdom of God unless he is born of water and the Spirit. Flesh gives birth to flesh, but the Spirit gives birth to spirit.

"You should not be surprised at my saying, You must be born again. The wind blows wherever it pleases. You hear its sound, but you cannot tell

> where it comes from or where it is going. So it is
> with everyone born of the Spirit."
>
> —John 3:1–7

Here Jesus makes the distinction between the flesh and the spirit.

> I declare to you, brothers that flesh and blood cannot
> inherit the kingdom of God, nor does the perishable
> inherit the imperishable. (1 Corinthians 15:50)

We all have to be transformed from the natural human into the spiritual human, and to accomplish this we are in need of a new beginning, a new birth with a different outcome. That can only happen with a new Father. And our new Father is God himself, eternal, immortal, imperishable, from everlasting to everlasting, never diminishing, never changing, and with the power to transform us into his likeness in Christ.

> He was in the world, and though the world was
> made through him, the world did not recognize
> him. He came to that which was his own, but his
> own did not receive him. Yet to all who received
> him, to those who believed in his name, he gave the
> right to become children of God—children born
> not of natural descent, nor of human decision, or
> a husband's will, but born of God. (John 1:10–13)

We who belong to Jesus Christ are eternal spiritual sons and daughters of God, living and ministering in and through a clay, dying, decaying corpse that is perishable and mortal. Every thought and action originating from it stinks as anything emanating from death would.

Years ago, the Lord showed me a deep spiritual truth using a potato. One afternoon as I was walking through our garden, the

Lord spoke to me and directed me to dig up a potato, which I promptly did. Then he said, "Cut it in half," which I also did. And then he began relating the potato to a born-again believer. The revelation was awesome!

Envision a potato growing down in the dirt. Potatoes grow underground with their stems breaking through to the sunlight and straining toward the sun. And we shall never be satisfied until we reach the Son.

The first thing I noticed about the potato was that the inside was pure and unaffected by the dirt, mud, bugs, grubs, and worms that lived around it. And the potato was in the dirt, the mud, and the earthen body but not part of it. The potato was easily removed because though it grew in the earth, it was not at all part of it. In fact, the potato was and is an alien and stranger in the earth.

Believers are like that potato. Though we live and grow within this body of death (dirt) with sin, temptation, and the like swirling about us like those worms, grubs, and other creatures, we are in no way part of it. Nor can these carnal bodies of walking, talking dirt in which we reside temporarily adversely affect our eternal destinations. Like the potato, when it is time to go, we are gone, and the dirt remains.

Whatever the dirt did is finished; the dirt's job is finished. The potato cannot be accountable or responsible for what the dirt did or failed to do. The potato had only one responsibility or job while living in the dirt, and that was to grow into a mature, fully developed potato.

However, even potatoes live and thrive among other potatoes! Potatoes are a family, and from one spud others grow. One bad, one compromised potato can affect the others, so that potato has a need for much prayer!

And this is what he promised us—even eternal life.
(1 John 2:25)

And this is the testimony: God has given us eternal life, and this life is in his Son. He who has the Son has life; he who does not have the Son of God does not have life. I write these things to you who believe in the name of the Son of God "so that you may know" that you have eternal life. (1 John 5:11–13)

For no matter how many promises God has made, they are "Yes" in Christ. And so through him the "Amen" is spoken by us to the glory of God. (2 Corinthians 1:20)